THE SELF-POISONERS

That's just another name for *us*, the general public. By smoking, driving, even breathing the air in our carpeted, heated, painted homes, we are exposing ourselves to a massive chemical assault that can wreck health in a staggering variety of ways. Dr. Sherry Rogers both reveals the full scope of poisons in our environment, shows how our bodies' detoxification system works to preserve us and explains how we can protect ourselves.

Sherry A. Rogers, M.D. is board certified by the American Academy of Family Practice and the American Academy of Environmental Medicine and is a fellow of the American College of Allergy and Immunology. She has presented her work at four international indoor air conferences, and lectured in six countries. Dr. Rogers teaches advanced courses in environmental medicine for physicians and was the editor of the environmental medicine columnn for *Internal Medicine World Report*, a publication reaching 100,000 physicians. Books by the author include: *Tired or Toxic?*, *The E.I. Syndrome*, *The E.I. Syndrome, Revised*, *The Cure Is in the Kitchen*, *You Are What You Ate*, *Macro Mellow*, *Wellness Against All Odds*, *The Scientific Basis of Selected Environmental Medicine Techniques*, and *Depression Is Not a Drug Deficiency*, all from Prestige Publishing of Syracuse, New York. At her private practice in environmental medicine and nutritional biochemistry in Syracuse, New York, 60 percent of her patients come from around the U.S. and the world. She also publishes a referenced quarterly newsletter for patients and physicians, which is available from Prestige Publishers, Box 3161, Syracuse, NY 13220, 1-800-846-ONUS or 315-455-7012.

Chemical Sensitivity

Environmental diseases and pollutants–how they hurt us, how to deal with them

Sherry A. Rogers, M.D.

Keats Publishing, Inc.  New Canaan, Connecticut

Chemical Sensitivity is not intended as medical advice. Its intent is solely informational and educational. Please consult a health professional should the need for one be indicated.

CHEMICAL SENSITIVITY

ISBN: 0-87983-634-2

24 DIG/DIG   15

Contents

THE CONCEPT OF CHEMICAL SENSITIVITY

We've all seen the incredible stories of chemical sensitivity in the newspapers, magazines, and television documentaries in the last 15 years: people who suddenly developed undiagnosable problems, who have to live out of doors to survive, who wear masks in public buildings, and are excluded from the environment. These are the exceptional cases, not the "walking wounded," many of whom are unaware that they are chemically sensitive. The numbers of people who are affected at both ends of this spectrum of disease are increasing rapidly, and their symptoms know no specialty boundaries. It thus becomes important for everyone to be able to recognize this great masquerader.

How the Tight or Sick Building Syndrome Was Born

The old adage "out of everything bad comes something good" could not have been more appropriate than it was for the formaldehyde fiasco of the late '70s, when thousands of homes were insulated with urea foam formaldehyde insulation (UFFI). The sudden addition of UFFI, which the body processes to formaldehyde, showed us how quickly chemical sensitivity can come about. After having pumped massive amounts of formaldehyde into the wall cavities of their homes, many people—literally overnight—developed a vast array of symptoms. After examining thousands of these cases, we quickly realized that this was a model for demonstrating *two important principles* of chemical sensitivity:

1. It can produce *any* symptom, in *any* person, at *any* time, but the brain is the most common target organ involved.
2. There is a vast range of individual susceptibility.

For example, one member of the household might have arthralgia (joint pains), mood swings, inability to concentrate, and be spacey, dizzy, and dopey. Another member would have a headache, nausea and flu-like achiness, while yet another would have depression with burning mucosal and respiratory passages. Two others could be totally unaffected.

As interest in formaldehyde increased, it was surprising to find that many buildings without UFFI had as high or higher levels of formaldehyde, especially the "tight" buildings (Gupta 1981). Many buildings, both new and existing, were retro-fitted or insulated and sealed to keep heat and air conditioning in, because of the energy crunch and the resulting need to conserve energy. Hence, the "tight" building syndrome was born.

Further research showed that many other foreign chemicals (called *xenobiotics*) were present in building materials and furnishings as well: toluene, xylene, hexanes, benzene, trichloroethane, styrene, phthalates, and pesticides (Feldman 1980). For example, a common carpet can outgas (release into the air) over half of the mentioned chemicals (EPA Report 1989). In response to the need for information, world conferences sprang up to bring together experts from all over the globe and research data grew exponentially (Canada 1990, Brasser 1989, Berglund 1988).

Treatment for some was simple avoidance, but others were less fortunate. They not only failed to recover but worsened; becoming reactive to many items that never before had bothered them, such as other chemicals, molds and even foods. Thus, a *third principle* was recognized:

3. The spreading phenomenon.

Exposure to one chemical produced susceptibility to other environmental components. We witnessed these three principles in action repeatedly. For example, in 1988, when the Environmental Protection Agency (EPA) installed new carpet in their offices, 126 out of 2000 workers became ill. There was a vast range of symptoms, with cerebral symptoms predominating. Some of the workers went on to develop a multitude of symptoms and have yet to recover.

Why Is Everyone Not Affected Equally?

The same question kept rearing its head: What determines who is affected and who is not? The answer: body chemistry. Somebody up there must have known we were going to eventually try to poison ourselves, so each of us has the ability to metabolize (or break down and get rid of) foreign chemicals (xenobiotics), a process known as *xenobiotic detoxication*. However, how well we perform this enormously complicated job depends on our genetic or inherited ability and on the extent of the environmental burden of chemicals challenging us. Knowledge of this process at a sub-cellular level—the molecular biochemistry—has enabled so many (including the author) to recover.

To simplify the process, xenobiotic detoxication can be thought of as occurring in two phases. Phase I takes place inside the cell (in the cytosol or cell fluid) and involves chemical processes (oxidation, reduction, and hydrolysis) that start to render the chemical less toxic to the body (Klaasen 1986).

For example, one of the primary components in phase I of the detoxication of ethanol is an enzyme, *alcohol dehydrogenase*. Since this enzyme requires a molecule of *zinc* in order to function, some patients who are zinc deficient cannot recover from the effects of alcohol until intracellular red blood cell zinc levels are measured, and corrected, if found to be deficient. How do we get zinc deficient? Easily. But of the many mechanisms, the self-selection of processed foods is high on the list.

Another important enzyme in phase I detoxication is aldehyde oxidase, which requires molybdenum, abundant in beans, an item no longer popular in the standard American diet (Elsborg 1983). You begin to readily appreciate how the processed foods of this century have decreased our ability to properly detoxify 21st century chemicals.

Phase II detoxication takes place inside the cell as well, along a chain of molecules called the cytochrome P-450 system. Found in the cellular membranes (the endoplasmic reticulum), the system carries out a process called *conjugation*. This is where chemical groups, including glutathione and other sulfur compounds, are attached to the offending chemical in order to detoxify it. The addition of these groups serves to increase its size, polarity (electric charge), and solubility so that it can be dragged out of the body and excreted in urine, sweat, or most commonly, stool (Caldwell 1983).

One major problem is that, molecule for molecule, the conjugate is lost forever. For example, for each molecule of pesticide (often imperceptibly odorless) that is conjugated with glutathione to be excreted in the stool, a molecule of glutathione (the conjugate) is also lost. It costs the body energy and nutrients in order to make glutathione. The bottom line is that *the work of detoxication uses up*, and loses forever, *energy and nutrients* in the process of detoxifying the chemicals that we breath and eat each day. But much of the time we are unaware of even being exposed to any chemicals.

THE TOTAL LOAD CONCEPT

A person with chemical susceptibility can become depleted of conjugates if he persists in living in an environment that overburdens his detoxication pathways. The man who has a headache and difficulty concentrating at work when using a particular solvent will be less likely to recover if he has recently painted or carpeted his home. His xenobiotic detoxication capacity may become overloaded and even exhausted. This is especially true if his nutrient status is marginal, as it can be with a diet of mainly processed foods and alcohol. All aspects of his lifestyle, then, become very important to his recovery.

One can quickly see how his alcohol consumption (also metabolized by this same phase I system using alcohol dehydrogenase and aldehyde dehydrogenase) becomes an important consideration—as well as the rest of his diet and environment—in determining how well he handles the chemical at work. Hence the concept of *total load* or total body burden becomes crucial to successful treatment. You can readily appreciate how parts of the currently operational medical model or paradigm need to be changed in order to successfully treat the victim of chemical sensitivity. *Chemical sensitivity does not follow the rules of drug-oriented medicine.*

Right now, drugs and surgery are the current mainstay of treatment for most disease. But give a drug (a foreign chemical that is metabolized by the same P-450 system) to a person with an already compromised system, and you make him worse. The already overloaded system is further stressed and new symptoms emerge. So treatment of these patients frustrates physicians whose only tools are drugs.

NUTRITIONAL STATUS IMPORTANT

In addition, it is not routine to check the status of nutrients, and it is still not part of the medical curriculum. But without this knowledge, one cannot fix what's broken in the xenobiotic detoxication pathway to render it more efficient in metabolizing chemicals. For example, magnesium is important in over 300 enzymes in the body, many of which are crucial in phase I and phase II detoxication. But food processing can substantially reduce the amount of magnesium and other minerals in a food. Going from brown rice to white rice, for example, reduces magnesium fivefold. In fact, a 1988 U.S. government study published in *Science News* (133:23, 356, 1988) shows that the average American diet provides only 40 percent of the daily requirement for magnesium.

Other studies revealed that over 51 percent of the people studied were magnesium deficient. In another study of 1033 hospitalized patients, 53 percent were found to be magnesium deficient, but 90 percent of the doctors never even ordered the test (Whang 1990). Of the 10 percent minority they did test, most doctors ordered the least sensitive indicators of magnesium status, namely an rbc (red blood cell) magnesium, or worse yet, a serum magnesium. Yet merely correcting a magnesium deficiency can improve one's chemical sensitivity, if this is his predominating deficiency (Rogers 1991).

We know that every airborne chemical in a room reaches an equilibrium in the blood of those people who are in the room. And a chemical odor does not have to be perceived in order to be in the blood or to cause a symptom. Odorless carbon monoxide can kill just as effectively as cyanide. But in the individual with a compromised detoxication system, ambient odorless *undetoxified xenobiotics can backlog and damage* regulatory enzymes and proteins. Alternate chemical processing pathways may be used, like the cytochrome P-448 system. However, this system can also convert the backlogged chemicals to carcinogens or more toxic chemicals than the original compound, or trigger the formation of autoantibodies (Parke 1987). Thus, when you fail to properly detoxify chemicals that you cannot even smell, they can backlog in the body and create new diseases, including cancer.

Genetic Changes

Undetoxified chemicals or xenobiotics can cause changes in the genetic material of cells, by several mechanisms, which in turn may lead to cancer. For example, zinc deficiency not only compromises the activity of phase I alcohol dehydrogenase, but also affects the components of the genetic machinery. Zinc is needed for the function of enzymes like RNA polymerase, necessary for the synthesis of proteins that regulate the genetic process. Another zinc-requiring enzyme is DNA polymerase, necessary for restoring the structure to the genetic helix after old, worn-out components have been replaced. Thymidine kinase is yet another zinc-dependent enzyme needed for proper gene repair. (For more information, see my book *Tired or Toxic?*) So with just *one mineral deficiency*, we have more than three additional *mechanisms to promote cancer*.

But that is not all. With a zinc deficiency, the metabolism of vitamins A and B6 suffers because the enzymes that convert them to useable forms (alcohol [retinol] dehydrogenase and pyridoxine kinase) are zinc-dependent. And so are many digestive enzymes (such as carbonic anhydrase) that are needed for proper nutrient absorption. The enzyme carboxypeptidase, necessary for protein metabolism, also requires zinc. So, if compromised by an undiagnosed zinc deficiency, the xenobiotic pathways requiring these zinc-dependent enzymes suffer; unmetabolized chemicals backlog and proceed to damage other xenobiotic metabolic pathways.

SPREADING PHENOMENON

When these new xenobiotic detoxication pathways are damaged, due to the backlog of unmetabolized chemicals, new chemicals are suddenly added to the list of those not tolerated. This is the *spreading phenomenon*, where once some individuals become chemically sensitized, they then start reacting to more and more chemicals that never before bothered them. This makes people who are unaware of the phenomenon doubt the sanity of the poor victim who is accused of faking it, being a hypochondriac, or malingering.

Now you can begin to appreciate how the worsening or spreading phenomenon can snowball, and we have glimpsed only a few enzymes and several minerals out of over 40 essential nutrients. Hence, another paradigm of medicine crumbles as we are better able to understand why a person can get worse even if removed from the initial chemical source. Removal is not enough; you must repair the biochemical damage.

As for the predominance of brain or cerebral symptoms, that is understandable considering most xenobiotics are hydrocarbons that are actually chemical solvents and are especially *lipophilic*. Lipophilic means they love lipids (fats) or fatty cell membranes. And, since the brain is full of lipids, this allows fast penetration of chemical fumes through the cribriform plate (inside at the top of the nose, which is also the base of the brain). The chemicals are able to quickly diffuse across cell membranes, into the brain, and into the blood. Actually, the brain or cerebral and neurologic effects of many xenobiotics are well-known.

Since, for example, pesticides cause predominantly CNS (central nervous system: the brain and spinal cord) and other neurological symptoms, it is not surprising that *pesticides are one of the main causes* or contributors to the emergence of chemical sensitivity. They are the perpetrators of the perfect crime, as they are ubiquitous and generally odorless. They can cause insidious or delayed, yet progressive symptoms even weeks after an exposure, once the threshold for an individual's tolerance is finally exceeded (Gershon 1961).

If the pesticides' innate toxicity (having been specifically designed as metabolic interrupters and neurotoxins, initially for chemical warfare) were not enough, many of the secondary metabolites (breakdown products) are even more toxic than the parent compounds. Recall that if the body cannot handle a chemical, sometimes it shifts to a chemical pathway that actually creates a carcinogen or another dangerous chemical. Some of these are toxic enough to damage the system, sometimes permanently, and in many cases the damage continues to progress, even though there is no further exposure. But worst of all, by their very nature as toxic and highly reactive compounds, pesticides are unstable enough to make finding any identifiable metabolites nearly impossible. Hence, as stated, they make the perfect crime.

DEBUNKING THE MYTH THAT "IT'S ALL IN YOUR HEAD"

It's obvious how important the total body burden of chemicals is to the overall picture presented to the clinician. For example, toluene is a chemical that we are all exposed to every day, as it commonly outgasses from paint, carpets, furnishings, plastics, adhesives like carpet glue, and much more. It can produce any symptom, but the most common target organ is the brain (EPA 1983). Benzene, a known cause of leukemia, also is a common environmental pollutant. You get a dose of it when you fill your car tank with gasoline, drive in heavy traffic (auto exhaust), go into a restroom with a strong deodorizer, or from rubber, solvents, and plastics. It also uses the brain as a favorite target organ.

But the presence of toluene in the blood slows or retards the metabolism of benzene, as they compete for the same enzymes in the detoxication system. Now you can begin to see how a person's mood swings, for example, can vary from day to day with exposure to the same chemical. We do not know precisely what the *total body burden* of toxins is at any one moment. This information is crucial, however, in determining how another chemical is metabolized at the same time. For the moment-to-moment metabolism of every substance is dependent upon all other substances that are being and have been metabolized.

For example, many xenobiotics, like trichloroethylene, if blocked from the normal phase I pathway, will form a secondary metabolite: *chloral hydrate* (the so-called "Mickey Finn" or knock-out drops). This explains symptoms such as the "brain fog" or the spacey, dopey, and dizzy behavior and inability to concentrate that wax and wane so prevalently. And if it weren't enough that this contributes to cerebral symptoms that leave the physician doubting the sanity of the patient, chloral hydrate is also mutagenic and procarcinogenic.

Furthermore, some xenobiotics can alter the blood-brain barrier, changing the penetration of other xenobiotics and nutrients into the brain (Halstead 1989). And again, when the P-450 system is too overloaded, metabolism can be shifted to the P-448 system where more toxic and often carcinogenic products are produced. As an example, other xenobiotics, like the pesticide dioxin, can fit into the DNA helix and cause it to bend and open up. This makes specific sites that were previously blocked accessible to other molecules, thereby turning on mechanisms for new diseases. Bearing this in mind, and the fact that Dr. Barbara McClintock received the 1984 Nobel Prize for showing that, in response to the environment, genes can "jump" from one locus (gene position) to another, it does not surprise us that some people seem forever changed after a specific environmental exposure.

There is also a phenomenon of *adaptation* where metabolism is shifted to other pathways so initial symptoms may appear to subside, only to have chronic disease or end-organ damage emerge elsewhere as a result. In other words, the body "gets used to" a certain chemical and learns how to adapt the chemistry to minimize symptoms. In doing so, however, the damage merely gets shifted to another target organ. In conventional medicine, every organ is treated by a different specialist. Symptoms in different target organs are not perceived as related to one another. Hence, to the uninitiated, the new disease erroneously appears to have nothing to do with previous events. More about this later.

THE ROLE OF DIET

Although nearly every cell has detoxication capabilities, those in the liver carry out a disproportionately large amount of this activity. Another major part of xenobiotic detoxication occurs in the lining of the gastrointestinal tract. Beneficial organisms that inhabit the gut also function as detoxicators. The wrong intestinal organisms, as well as xenobiotics from food additives, pesticides and preservatives can jeopardize the integrity of these pathways in the gut. So these are traditional reasons why attention to the diet is essential for successfully treating chemical sensitivity.

For example, you have learned that Phase II of detoxication involves hooking a conjugate or large molecule onto the foreign chemical so that it becomes polar and heavy and can be dragged out into the gut from the liver. So when a molecule of glucuronide conjugates a plasma xenobiotic, an energy-requiring process, the resulting xenobiotic-glucuronide complex is excreted into the bowel and eliminated. However, the intestinal organisms of people on a high meat diet can hydrolyze the complex (or rip this conjugate off the chemical), using the enzyme B-glucuronidase made by intestinal bacteria. Then the naked xenobiotic can be reabsorbed into the bloodstream.

The metabolic work of conjugation is thus wasted. The glucuronide is lost forever, and the body is in a negative state in relation to energy and detoxication nutrients. The original xenobiotic is back in the blood to deal with. So for most people, healing is facilitated by avoiding diets high in meat. Diets high in cruciferous vegetables (cabbage, broccoli, etc.) and specific essential fatty acids can enhance intestinal metabolism of potent xenobiotics.

Additives also may jeopardize xenobiotic metabolism by other mechanisms in addition to overloading the enzymes. For example, tartrazine (a yellow food dye used to make a loaf of bread look as if it were made with eggs) can lower the zinc status. The zinc deficiency can then snowball as many of its 90 dependent enzymes become compromised, as described earlier. As well, some individuals ferment dietary carbohydrates (like sugars and starches) to ethanol. This ethanol, which is alcohol, not only competes for the phase I alcohol dehydrogenase, but can cause secondary intestinal epithelial (gut lining) inflammation which further compromises the integrity of the intestinal P-450 system (Hunnisett 1990).

Even with these limited examples, it is obvious that diet plays no small role in an individual's speed of recovery, and no less a role in his susceptibility to chemical backlog and additional symptoms. The major food to eliminate from the diet to improve xenobiotic metabolism is sugar. Through a process of non-enzymatic glycosylation, sugars can attach to regulatory proteins and enzymes and alter their function just like any xenobiotic.

MOLECULAR MEDICINE—AN IDEA WHOSE TIME HAS COME

We haven't touched on even one-tenth of the detoxication mechanisms, nor even mentioned free radical pathology and lipid peroxidation, but both topics have received excellent coverage in other works in this Good Health Guide series. But we have truly entered the era of molecular medicine. Past models or paradigms upon which the practice of medicine is based interfere with our comprehension of the mechanisms of chemical sensitivity.

There are three main reasons necessitating a paradigm shift and for simultaneously ushering us into the era of molecular medicine:

1. We are the first generation of people to ever be exposed on a daily basis to such an unprecedented number of chemicals. For many, the home environment is worse than their occupational environment. In the past, it would not be unusual for a building to have a complete exchange of air with outside air every few hours. Now

some buildings may go days or weeks before this occurs. A study of 600 office workers in the USA showed that 20 percent experienced symptoms of sick building syndrome. A World Health Organization report estimates that 30 percent of the people in new and refurbished buildings worldwide are affected by the syndrome.

2. There is an unprecedented amount of work for the xenobiotic detoxication system of new-21st-century man, due to the processing of foods and changes in dietary preferences. There is also a decline in the nutrients upon which these pathways depend. Examples include going from whole-grain foods to those made with bleached white flour. Such processing results in a significant loss of vitamin E, whose purpose is to sit in cell membranes and guard against the entry of xenobiotics that damage intracellular mechanisms. Another example is that hydrogenated oils (such as margarines and cooking fats) contain trans fatty acids. The fatty acids are processed in this way to make them solid at room temperature. However, these molecules can actually inhibit the enzyme (delta-6-desaturase) necessary for the metabolism of essential fatty acids in the cell endoplasmic reticulum where detoxication occurs.

3. Xenobiotics can deplete or exhaust nutrients by a variety of mechanisms. The resultant deficiencies determine which enzymes are compromised and consequently which xenobiotics are improperly metabolized. No wonder that blood analysis can be practically like a fingerprint. It can literally identify where a person has been. For example, elevated levels of benzene can be measured after being in a service station, a dry cleaning establishment, or around new paint, the EPA noted in 1987. But the damage caused by the delayed persistence of these chemicals in the body, which is in part determined by the detoxication integrity, is what determines chemical susceptibility.

Even though common sense would dictate that removal

from the offending xenobiotic should end the problem, many people continue to get worse. In the EPA study mentioned above, four weeks after the carpet had been installed, the levels of 4-phenylhexane, styrene and toluene were less than half the original levels. But with a less-than-healthy detox system to begin with, and one that is working to capacity just to keep up with the daily total body burden of xenobiotics from multiple sources, four weeks of exposure is more than enough to accumulate a backlog of toxic chemicals and their metabolites. This in turn can proceed to irreparable damage that persists and continues to snowball. In addition, many of these products are carcinogenic.

Without being able to rely on drugs, treating chemical sensitivity can be very frustrating for the clinician. Never before in the history of medicine has one disease necessitated the combined roles of assessing the nutrient status, diet, and environment of the patient in order to help him heal. As we enter the era of molecular medicine, no longer is a headache an aspirin deficiency. We have broken the paralyzing paradigm of using drugs to treat (or merely mask the symptoms of) all illnesses.

DIAGNOSIS AND TREATMENT OF CHEMICAL SENSITIVITY

Throughout the history of science, man has found it difficult to accept new paradigms. A paradigm is merely a temporary model to explain observations. It survives only until science proves that it is outdated. Remember that Semmelweis, the Hungarian obstetrician, was banned from his medical society just for recommending that physicians wash their hands between autopsies and obstetrical deliveries. Although his patients had a markedly higher survival rate due to reductions in fatal puerperal fever, his ideas were not accepted until long after his death.

NEW RULES OF MEDICINE ARE NEEDED

Before the old paradigms can be discarded, physicians need to be aware of some key concepts regarding chemical sensitivity:

1. Human beings have a tremendous genetic polymorphism and biochemical heterogeneity. In other words, we not only look different from one another on the outside, we are biochemically and genetically unique on the inside. As a result, any symptom can be a manifestation of chemical sensitivity and any target organ is vulnerable.
2. Because the total body burden of environmental stressors is never the same at any two moments, symptoms may not only fluctuate, but may appear inconsistent with exposure. Thus, the standard "double-blind" studies and repeated exposure trials are almost impossible to do.
3. Although there are common constellations of symptoms, no two patients are alike in either symptom causes or requirements for recovery.
4. In the chemically sensitive individual, there are multiple defects or deficiencies in the xenobiotic (foreign chemical) detoxication system. These individuals are then reactive to chemicals at levels where others are seemingly unaffected.
5. Chemicals can cause damage to the system that is silently cumulative, e.g., a single pack of cigarettes does not cause cancer, but over time the effects add up.
6. Once this system becomes overloaded and unable to handle the incoming load, further exposures cause a backup of undetoxified metabolites, which then go on to damage other regulatory enzymes and proteins.

Hence, we have the spreading phenomenon whereby the victim now becomes reactive to xenobiotics that never before bothered him. This leaves those unfamiliar with the biochemistry of xenobiotic detoxication doubting the motives and sanity of the victim.

The Old Way

The recipe for the usual approach to many current medical problems is to do a history, a physical and a laboratory workup. Then a diagnosis is made, which dictates a specific treatment, usually drugs, to suppress or stifle symptoms (i.e., anticolitis drugs, antiarrhythmia drugs, antiarthritis drugs, etc). Often, after longstanding drug suppression has ceased to be effective, surgery is the recourse. The malfunctioning part is cut away, thrown out, and replaced: colectomy, coronary bypass, total hip replacement.

When symptoms are suppressed with drugs, the actual cause is usually not sought, so the patient inevitably goes on to develop other symptoms related to the initial dysfunction. But because medical care is fragmented, no one physician appreciates the change in the target organ as one symptom is suppressed and another emerges.

For example, the cardiologist may consider it of little importance that his patient with recalcitrant palpitations or arrhythmia also sees an orthopedist for chronic lumbosacral pain or has irritable bowel syndrome, or depression or fatigue. But all of these are common magnesium deficiency symptoms. (Recall that the U.S. government survey reveals that the average American diet provides only 40 percent of the daily requirement for magnesium; that there is no blood test that will accurately rule it out; and also many doctors do not think to check.)

If chronic back spasm or diarrhea is caused by a magnesium deficiency in an individual, but an antispasmodic is prescribed instead, the deficiency goes undiagnosed. When the patient then begins a recalcitrant arrhythmia, antiarrhythmia drugs are used. The final sudden death by cardiac arrest still can fail to spark the suspicion that the opportunity to actually cure all of the problems was missed. Instead, the problem snowballed. If the patient had a concomitant formaldehyde sensitivity from the new carpet also contributing to his arrhythmia, this further decreases the likelihood of all the causes ever being discovered.

The diagnosis of chemical sensitivity proceeds in an entirely different fashion, probably primarily because there are no drugs to completely eradicate the symptoms. To give another chemical to an already compromised xenobiotic detoxication system just does not work. So the physician is forced to find the cause.

THE CAUSES OF DISEASE

Let's look at the causes of disease. They can be:

1. **GENETIC,** as with inborn errors or enzyme defects like phenylketonuria (PKU), where the enzyme to metabolize the common dietary amino acid, phenylalanine is missing, or AHH (aryl hydroxylase hydratase) deficiency, or the inability to detoxify debrisoquine (an antimalarial drug), leading to Parkinsonism (Barbeau 1985), or the fact that women have a decreased ability for detoxication compared with men (Frezza 1990).

2. **PSYCHOGENIC,** like some cases of anxiety, or sudden death in previously healthy, recently widowed people. Included in this category are any of the vast array of psychoneuroimmune phenomena. In such cases, actual nutrient deficiencies and immune changes can be precipitated by thoughts of grief, anxiety, anger, and depression via our own neurotransmitters.

3. **ENVIRONMENTAL** agents, internal or external. Some of the components of environmental causes include: (a) trauma, such as being hit by a truck, (b) infection (current drug-oriented medicine is excellent here), or (c) metabolic/endocrine/autoimmune diseases, like diabetes or thyroiditis. Many of these disorders are progres-

sively being found to have environmental triggers (Prilipko 1983, Rea 1992).

Environmental symptoms can also be (d) food-induced, like forms of arthritis or the gas, bloating and diarrhea from lactase deficiency. Food intolerances may manifest as hypercholesterolemia, irritable bowel syndrome (Mullin 1991), or arteriosclerosis. Plant lectin-induced malabsorption, or celiac disease from wheat intolerance can also produce symptoms. Other food symptoms can manifest as migraine, colitis, milk-induced hypochlorhydria (low stomach acid) with resultant nutrient deficiencies (Kokkonen 1979), or learning disability, or monosodium glutamate (MSG)-induced retinal deterioration.

Environmental illness can also be (e) chemically induced, as with a simple irritant cough from cigarettes, to complex antigen production from the plasticizers TMA (trimellitic anhydride) and TDI (toluene diisocyanate), or systemic sclerosis from dry cleaning fluid (Lockey 1987). Ubiquitous chemicals like formaldehyde from new home construction can trigger chronic fatigue or headache. Common hydrocarbons from auto exhaust can trigger glomerulonephritis. Workplace solvents can trigger panic disorder (Dager 1987), or dry cleaning fluid-induced cardiac toxicity (Mago 1981), or typewriter correction fluid-induced sudden cardiac death.

Chemicals can mimic hormones and act as chemical messengers to rearrange genes. Chemically induced symptoms resulting from subacute chronic pesticide poisoning range from the classic inability to concentrate, irritability, and depression (Levin 1976), to nausea, abdominal pain, tremor, headaches, and paresthesias. Less frequently observed are pancreatitis (IMWR 1989) or unexplained death, to the more insidious symptoms of poor memory, frank schizophrenia (Gershon 1961) or inability to concentrate.

Other such conditions include benzene-induced leukemia, heavy metal toxicity with deteriorating IQ, cardiac arrhythmia induced by carpet adhesive, as well as autoimmunity, and some forms of vasculitis or thrombophlebitis (Rea

1978b). In essence, many of *the basic pathologies of disease can be triggered by any number of everyday chemicals and foods.*

Symptoms can be triggered by (f) pollen, dust, mold and mite allergies. These often unsuspected substances can contribute to, or be the sole cause of: chronic asthma, headaches, fatigue, and nasal congestion; or (g) toxins, such as mycotoxins from ubiquitous everyday molds that can mimic every symptom of chemical sensitivity, including cancer. There are numerous other environmental factors such as (h) sunlight in seasonal affective disorder; (i) electromagnetic field (EMF)-induced spontaneous abortions and leukemia in animals and people living near high voltage lines that emit these fields; (j) radon-induced lung cancer; (k) temperature/humidity-induced symptoms; or (l) the effects of negative ions, e.g. causing depression; or (m) irritants like asbestos (mesothelioma or pericarditis) (IMWR 1991).

4. **NUTRIENT DEFICIENCIES** such as vitamin B12 deficiency causing neuropsychiatric disorders without anemia or macrocytosis, or without paresthesias, or mimicking multiple sclerosis. Vitamin B12 deficiency may also cause an inability to properly metabolize cholesterol, or contribute to chronic asthma. Dietary choline deficiency (a B vitamin) causes memory loss.

Unsuspected mineral deficiencies such as zinc or magnesium contribute directly to the inability to metabolize everyday chemicals or to the mixed symptoms of chronic fatigue syndrome (Cox 1991), or premenstrual syndrome. Magnesium deficiency can mimic organic brain syndrome, just as chromium deficiency can contribute to the pathology of arteriosclerosis (Boyle 1977).

Obviously, many conditions are combinations of causes (like chronic fatigue syndrome, acquired immunodeficiency syndrome, cancer, arteriosclerosis, schizophrenia, and of course, chemical sensitivity). This is a fortunate situation. Even if one cause is immutable with our current techniques, other aspects of the total load can be changed significantly to bring about wellness. For example, in the person with the genetically determined disease PKU, the accumulation of unmetabolized products leads to death. But even though we can't yet change the genetics, the condition can be corrected with a diet free of phenylalanine.

Similarly, formaldehyde-induced throat spasms can sometimes be controlled by simply correcting the underlying magnesium deficiency that makes the spasms possible in the first place. The total load concept works both ways: The victim must have the genetic predisposition for the throat to be the target organ and a nutrient deficiency to make spasms possible. There must also be an environmental overload to that particular target organ at that time. If some components of the total load burden are missing, the person no longer exhibits symptoms when exposed to traffic exhaust or whatever the formaldehyde source was.

Environmental medicine is based on finding the causes for all symptoms. And there is increasingly more evidence for a gradual shift to environmental medicine. As one example, conventional treatment of high blood pressure with medication can actually cause a rise in lipids (*New England Journal of Medicine*, Sept. 28, 1989), while other studies show that with nutrient corrections and no medications, blood pressure can be successfully treated.

Free Radical Pathology as the Mechanism of Disease

A complete description of free radical pathology is not possible here, but a simplification may help in understanding this subject. Suppose a man is tanking up his car with gasoline. He is also absorbing benzene from the gasoline through his lungs. The chemical is in the bloodstream in measurable amounts within minutes. In order for the body to begin to detoxify it, phase I reactions begin. There are multiple routes, not merely one set pathway, for detoxication. However, in phase I reactions, a charged particle called an electron is usually lost from a molecule (Reilly 1991, Levine 1985).

Normally, electrons, which orbit the atoms in a molecule,

are paired. When a free radical, a molecule with a single electron, is created, this unpaired electron is always seeking another to balance it. It is highly reactive and highly destructive and will do anything to try to rip the missing electron from anything in its path. Usually the first thing in its path are cell enzymes and cell membranes. These membranes are analogous to the computer keyboard, as they dictate what goes on within the cell. They regulate calcium channels, letting calcium in and out of cells, and also the sodium pump. The membranes provide access to the genetic material, make up the endoplasmic reticular membranes (where xenobiotic detoxication takes place), etc. As membranes get destroyed over the years by these single-electron free radicals, often the accumulated effect or weakness predominates in one particular organ, like the heart, for example. We patch up the symptoms with calcium channel blockers, diuretics, digitalis, chemotherapy, tranquilizers, etc. The result we call a chronic disease, which eventually results in end organ failure and death.

Of course, the body has a system of checks and balances to control this mechanism of aging and degeneration. For example, one of the roles of vitamin C in the blood plasma is to act as the first line of defense as a free radical quencher, stopping that wildly destructive molecule in its tracks (Padh 1991, Frei 1989). If that fails, vitamin E sits in the cell wall (membrane) and grabs the chemical as it tries to enter the cell and create further destruction in its attempt to find a mate for its lonesome electron (Linder 1984).

Obviously if these two nutrients, C and E, are deficient (as in a typical diet of fast foods and missed meals), or have been used up by too many other chemical exposures, the defenses are weak. But this explanation is a simplification, and many xenobiotics are powerful metabolic uncouplers which can initiate a cascade, backwards as well as forward, of progressively destructive reactions.

It gets more complicated when you know that we need adequate vitamin C to regenerate to a reduced state (or usable form again) minerals used in normal and detoxication reactions. We also need vitamin C to restore used vitamin

E and recycle it to restore its antioxidant ability. In other words, it has become recycled and is now able to be used again in its own function as a protector of cell walls and membranes. But when the defenses are so strong that free radicals are neutralized quickly, there is a tremendous reduction in stress to the system. It is then able to concentrate on the work of healing instead of just everyday adaptation.

ADAPTATION RESULTS IN CHRONIC DISEASE

Chronic disease is the price we pay for chronic adaptation. It also makes it abundantly clear why attention to the total body burden or total load of stressors is so important to the diagnosis and treatment of chemical sensitivity. In fact, *the diagnosis is often the treatment.* For in looking at the possible contributors to the total load, as one whittles away at them, the load diminishes and the patient begins to recover. But all this new knowledge is necessary to make the diagnosis. We can no longer just do a blood test and X-ray and prescribe a pill. The old rules do not work.

Compare this method with current medicine, where a diagnosis connotes a recipe for a pharmaceutical protocol. You can understand why the patient can be like an accident waiting to happen. Symptoms are *masked* with drugs, rather than determining the underlying environmental and biochemical causes and correcting them. There is only one thing that can then happen: *The sick get sicker.*

Seven Principles

There are seven principles of environmental medicine:

1. Biochemical individuality
2. Total load
3. Spreading phenomenon
4. Adaptation

5. De-adaptation
6. Bipolarity
7. Switch phenomenon

The first three have been discussed earlier.

Adaptation is what happens when a person is exposed to an agent, such as a chemical. The body detoxication system must compensate for greater metabolic needs. There is *enzyme induction*: Hepatic (liver) enzymes specific for metabolizing the chemical begin to work and additional enzymes are made. Energy is expended in the process. In some cases, as for phenobarbital ingestion, the induced enzymes can then speed the metabolism of other drugs going through the system.

Once new enzymes are induced, there is a new *set point*. The body does not react as it did to the same stimulus or substance; in fact it sometimes fails to react at all, giving the false impression that the agent is no longer harmful. An example is alcohol tolerance, whereby a person adapts to increasing amounts over a period of time. However, with the synthesis of adaptive enzymes and the resultant new set point, there may now be an onset of new symptoms from that same stimulus. But because they are different, they may not be recognized as having anything to do with the original stimulus.

Likewise, there is what appears to be de-adaptation, which has a number of biochemical explanations. One example is phenol, a common preservative in all allergy injections and many other medications. It is also found in many construction materials, home and office furnishings and cleaning solutions. The detoxication components in the body usually pick up phenol readily, but they cannot process large amounts. After a brief honeymoon where it is effectively detoxed, phenol then becomes a problem as the enzymes are used up and the process is shifted to other chemical pathways (where it may be inadequately metabolized).

Likewise, other xenobiotics can exhaust certain pathways and cease to be handled in the original fashion. The result is that now a person may react to a chemical that never before bothered her (Rea 1978a). One can readily see why failure to comprehend this basic biochemistry can make chemical sensitivity appear to be a psychiatric disease.

Bipolarity is the sixth phenomenon, which merely means that the same agent can sometimes cause a stimulus reaction and at other times cause a depressive reaction. The outcome depends on dose, time frame, and the action of adaptive enzymes. Alcohol is a good example. At first it acts as a stimulant, but later when converted into the aldehyde phase, the depressive reaction follows. It is important for the physician to be aware that *many* foods and chemicals cause these dual reactions, making diagnosis more challenging.

The switch phenomenon is the last principle, whereby the target organ can easily switch from one to another. A simple example is an asthmatic person with colitis or schizophrenia who will rarely have all target organs symptomatic at one time. Rather, when one disease process is active, the other is quiescent, and vice versa. This is why it really is of secondary importance what the symptoms are: *It is the cause that counts.* *All* diseases of an individual must be considered if she is going to arrive at a state of wellness.

THE DIAGNOSIS IS PART OF THE TREATMENT

Studies today show that over one-third of physicians do an inferior medical history. Subsequent diagnoses of the patient rely on the diagnosis derived from this history. Diagnosis of the chemically sensitive patient also begins with the patient's history, yet goes far beyond that taken in general medicine. For example, in taking an environmental medicine history, drugs are not looked at as beneficial. They are viewed as potentially contributing to symptoms because of their cumulative biochemical effect, and their known ability to cause specific nutrient deficiencies.

For instance, diuretics (used for fluid retention and high

blood pressure) are notorious for causing hypokalemia (low potassium). But diuretics also cause magnesium deficiency, which may even be the cause of the problem (e.g., hypertension) for which the diuretic was prescribed in the first place. The magnesium deficiency can then promote lipidemia and D-6-D (delta-6-desaturase) deficiency (a crucial enzyme in the metabolism of essential fatty acids), and further damage the endoplasmic reticular membranes, where detoxication takes place. If that were not enough, diuretics themselves can promote lipidemia as well as thiamine (vitamin B1) deficiency. These in turn can contribute to a decline in cardiac performance: another example of spreading phenomenon. *The sick get sicker* when drugs are used to hide symptoms.

The enlightened physician looks for adverse effects of currently prescribed foods and medications. For example, margarines and hydrogenated polyunsaturated oils, often recommended as substitutes for butter, can contain as much as 35 percent trans fatty acids. This type of fatty acid produces long-ranging damage to membranes (Mensink 1990). Or consider the case of the number-one type of prescribed drug, the H2 inhibitors (like cimetidine and ranitidine for stomach ulcers). By inhibiting gastric acid secretion, these drugs decrease absorption of essential detox vitamins and minerals. Nonsteroidal anti-inflammatory drugs known as NSAIDs (like ibuprofen), increase intestinal permeability, and actually promote food allergy (Bjarnson 1984) and autoimmunity. Thus, they promote the pathophysiology—the very thing that caused the condition in the first place. As mentioned earlier, the yellow food and medicine dye, tartrazine, found in foods, and also in the outer covering of prescribed medications, can promote zinc deficiency. The antihypertensive medication hydralazine, meant to reduce the damage of the arteriosclerosis, has a side effect: it promotes pyridoxine (vitamin B6) deficiency, which in turn promotes arteriosclerosis (Feuer 1990).

For the chemically sensitive, antibiotics are not looked at only for their allergic potential. Their ability to upset the normal balance in intestinal flora, thereby causing malabsorption with resultant nutrient deficiencies in the detox pathways, is also considered.

A history of self-prescribed vitamin/mineral supplementation is also needed, since many formulations actually promote deficiencies by the nature of their imbalance. For example, a person may take zinc to bolster his immune system. But this alone can cause a copper deficiency that impairs the ability to detoxify chemicals, or can lead to chronic fatigue or depression.

A good history includes a determination of work (Feldman 1980) and home exposures to xenobiotics, and identifies when and where symptoms are improved. In some cases, symptoms appear within one to three years of having moved into a renovated office or brand new home. Knowledge of the diet in detail, symptoms in relation to meals and fasting, and even the method of preparation of foods is important, as it greatly alters the detoxication capabilities.

A dental and surgical history, including the nature of the reparative materials used, is also necessary. Many chemically sensitive people begin experiencing symptoms shortly after root canal, surgery or anesthesia (Rea 1987a).

It is important to know when they were last really well, what their lifestyle was at that time, as well as any stresses. A plethora of minutia needs to be sifted through in regard to hobbies, hidden pesticides, local industry, traffic, home furnishings, cooking utilities, and other potent and common causes of debilitating symptoms.

In regard to symptoms, most people are eager to admit that it is the first time they have been asked about mental symptoms of the classic brain fog, for example: confusion, inability to concentrate, fatigue, mood swings, poor memory, unwarranted depression, spaciness, or dizziness. They say that most specialists hearing these complaints were unconcerned with such details, which did not relate to their field of expertise. When patients did dare tell of them, psychiatric referral was recommended.

To make connections between symptoms that cross specialty lines is essential for the physician trained in taking an environmental medicine history. For example, if someone with eye muscle twitches or leg cramps, being treated for chronic back problems, and having arrhythmia or palpitations becomes chemically sensitive, he is most assuredly magnesium deficient. Of course, this deficiency impairs the detox capabilities.

In regard to physical signs, often there are none. And those that are present are usually not reflected in the multiple reports of physicals that patients bring with them. Common findings, previously unnoticed, may be: a white furry or coated tongue (after several courses of antibiotics) dark areas under the eyes, white spots and splitting of the nails, swelling, skin temperature, broken blood vessels, dry skin and hair, not enough teeth for proper mastication, amalgams (Stortebecker 1986), and mixed oral metals, unusual body odors, abnormal eye muscle movements, poor focusing, poor recent memory, and even the inability to stand on one leg or on tip-toes with eyes closed (commonly lost with pesticide exposures).

If the examining physician's office is not chemically clean, he or she may witness a chemical sensitivity reaction firsthand: The patient's eyes will get glassy and his cheeks and/or ears will flush. The person may become progressively more nasty, forgetful, spacey, depressed or otherwise difficult and frustrating to obtain a history from. Some of the more common immediate vascular signs, manifest as flushing, edema, blanching or cold extremities, with varying degrees of cerebral (brain) incompetence. It is quite common for the person with a magnesium deficiency, for example, to have a very cold handshake. This is a mere cursory sampling to show that detection of chemical sensitivity requires an extensive history and physical exam with extra detail and an environmental and biochemical focus.

Laboratory workup likewise begins where the current conventional workup leaves off. Many of the items are common sense. For example, any patient who does not awaken feeling great, and especially one with symptoms of headache, nasal congestion, recurrent sinusitis or post-nasal drip, bronchitis or asthma, should have an exposed petri dish in the bedroom. This clear dish, with a removable cover, contains a solid nutrient base (culture media) upon which microorganisms can grow. Exposure will show whether molds are present in the room and may be causing symptoms. It is particularly important for asthmatics who awaken in the wee hours of the morning with symptoms, to expose the plate at that time. To expose it in the day will only pick up the fungi that are prevalent then, and not the causative ones that sporulate in large numbers at night when symptoms are triggered.

My experience has shown that the choice of the culture media is no small matter either, since 30 percent more fungi are isolated when the proper one is used (Rogers 1984). Likewise, it is important to culture the first morning sputum of asthmatics, especially when they have been on antibiotics, and oral or inhaled steroids.

Bowel studies are important to rule out unsuspected inflammation (Jackson 1981) and malabsorption with insufficient digestive protein breakdown, abnormal flora, insufficient beneficial flora, or improper chewing, due to poor teeth. Study of the bowel flora, is of course important since these organisms play a role in metabolizing vitamins, drugs, hormones, carcinogens, and xenobiotics (Gorbach 1986).

Quantitative measurement of immunoglobulin levels, hormone analyses, such as a testosterone, serotonin, progesterone, or DHEA (dehydroepiandrosterone, an adrenal hormone) in cases of depression, or the cortrosyn stimulation test (Jeffries 1981), or magnesium loading test (Rogers 1991a) in cases with chronic fatigue, have often been exceedingly useful. In both cases, for the most severely damaged patients, T and B cell measurements, iris recorder analysis (Rea 1992), and much more are needed. It must be remembered at all times that *no two patients are the same.*

Testing by specialty laboratories for pesticides and other xenobiotics and their metabolites, as well a heavy metal stimulation test may demonstrate underlying metabolic poisons that can forever inhibit normal metabolism until they are discovered and cleared.

The inability of a person to metabolize chemicals in a particular environment can be demonstrated with before and after blood and urine tests, i.e., Monday morning before work, and Thursday evening after a week of exposure. Skin testing done using the conventional double-blind method, can provoke and prove symptom causation (Rogers 1987), as will "booth" challenges done with any antigen: molds, pollens, foods, chemicals, hormones, etc. In this type of testing, people are put in a chemically clean testing booth and various antigens are pumped in to determine if they bring about symptoms.

Nutrient level determinations are particularly important. For example, chromium and carnitine levels must be checked in the person with chronic fatigue who also craves sweets. With deficiencies in these nutrients, such individuals cannot get the needed nutrients into their cells, regardless of how much they eat. Sometimes, however, these deficiencies are only part of the cause. Intense cravings, which may be the only early warning signs, suggest that there are biochemical deficiencies.

Intracellular zinc should also be measured in the chemically sensitive patient, I've found. Recall that alcohol dehydrogenase, a phase I xenobiotic detoxication enzyme, is zinc dependent. Intracellular molybdenum is required for the function of the enzyme aldehyde oxidase. Without this enzyme, there will be a biochemical bottleneck for detox when the total load gets too high. Molybdenum is also important in the enzyme sulfite oxidase, which is why some sulfite sensitive asthmatics lose their "sensitivity" when the molybdenum deficiency is corrected. Other such patients may have different biochemical defects.

When a sulfite sensitivity appears, we may forget to ask what in the environment changed to bring this about. It is known, for example, that phenol (in cleaning solutions, allergy injections, etc.) and pentachlorophenol (a common wood preservative) both inhibit the enzyme sulfite oxidase. It is exciting that there now appear to be biochemical and environmental explanations for many diseases.

Some nutrients, like magnesium or vitamin B12, should be used on a trial basis. There can be deficiencies even in spite of a normal blood test. Obviously, the various intracellular minerals that are most commonly low and most importantly found in the detox pathway are checked first. Mineral deficiencies take longer to correct as often new enzymes that incorporate them must be formed. Later, if needed, checks can be made of levels of selected vitamins, amino acids and fatty acids, all of which have vital roles in detoxication pathways. A knowledge of the patient's history (such as described above) helps the physician be more selective in ordering these nutrient analyses.

PATIENT EDUCATION IS THE KEY

In environmental medicine, there is also a major emphasis on patient education. When segments of the basic diagnostic process (e.g., avoidance of offending substances) are also included in the treatment, this is in part possible only because the patient has been educated (Rapp 1991, Rogers 1986, Rousseau 1987). *He or she must learn how to reduce the total load enough to see (by experiencing a reduction in symptoms), that he or she is on the right track.* Patients must also be able to see for the first time that there are not only causes for their symptoms, but that they have a major role in determining whether or not the symptoms are manifested.

The patient has the most intimate knowledge of his lifestyle, since major influences on his health come from the diet, office and home environments. He is therefore the logical one to make many of the diagnostic correlations that can then later be verified.

TREATMENT

As with conventional allergies, avoidance and environmental controls are paramount in treatment. This approach is much more complex, necessitating a thorough knowledge of environmental medicine by the patient as well as the physician. For example, gone are the smelly plastic mattress covers, foam pillows, waterbeds and air cleaners with particle board cabinets that we all recommended when we did conventional allergy treatment. We now know that they outgas phenols and formaldehyde that accentuate the patient's symptoms, producing morning irritability, headache or an inability to think straight. (Rogers 1986).

Since the patient spends a third of his life in the bedroom, we like to create an oasis that allows him to be symptom-free. My books explain the technique for mold plate exposure; describe air-cleaning devices that remove dusts, molds, and chemicals; and give the rationale for removal of as many materials that outgas xenobiotics as possible. This is to allow him to awaken for the first time with reduced symptoms.

Another major factor that can markedly reduce symptoms in the chemically sensitive is diet. Conventional allergists seem to concentrate on IgE-induced food allergy (an immune system reaction), but that plays a smaller role in chemical sensitivity. It is overshadowed by many nonimmunological mechanisms of food intolerance that have a profound influence on symptoms, such as inflammation (Teahon 1991), nutrient depletion and abnormal gut flora.

In spite of tremendous individual variation, there are some fairly common food intolerances worthy of mention. Physicians with no training in environmental medicine, but who are aware of these offenders, can make a profound improvement in the quality of life for many patients. For example, many patients with various forms of longstanding severe arthritis are amazed to find they have a vast reduction in pain after abstaining from all red meat and from foods in the Nightshade family (potatoes, tomatoes, peppers, eggplant, chili, paprika and tobacco) *for three months.* Many have a vast reduction in chronic nasal and chest congestion if they discontinue all milk products and wheat. Ferments (bread, cheese, vinegar, catsup, mustard, mayonnaise, salad dressing, alcohol, chocolate, and anything else aged, pickled or fermented) and sugar are common causes of fatigue and depression.

For many milder forms of chemical sensitivity, a diet change may be all that is necessary, but unfortunately by the time one is prescribed, the patient's sensitivities have usually increased. But early on, diet is the most effective remedy and requires no expensive tests, just patient education. Early dietary intervention would be a very cost-effective measure for all physicians to learn to administer. Many recalcitrant conditions, like chronic prostatitis and vaginitis, colitis, arthritis and others, are often markedly improved if the hidden food intolerances are identified. Intradermal food testing can be done if injections are needed for more difficult cases (King 1988a,b; Miller 1987b; Rapp 1978, Rea 1984).

Even though many patients tell us that their chronic sinusitis, bronchitis, hay fever, headache or asthma are not their main reasons for coming (in fact they had endured these miseries for years without concern), they are a necessary part of the total load. Often patients are surprised to find that what appeared to be chemical sensitivity was really dust/mold allergy (Rogers 1991). However, because they are often more sensitive to dust and molds (compared to the average allergic person without complaint of chemical sensitivity), we find that they require careful individual fine-tuning or titration of their inhalant injection doses (King 1987, Nalebuff 1988).

It is imperative that these supersensitive individuals not be overloaded by chemical preservatives in their injections that may make them more reactive. Hence, these chemicals are tested first (Rogers 1987). Phenol, the standard preservative in allergy injections, is not only a known carcinogen, but has a predilection for the brain and is immunosuppressive (Nour-Eldin 1970, LaVia 1979).

There are also many newer molds that have been researched and found to be the hidden cause of symptoms (Rogers 1991b). It is important that the more severely afflicted be tested for exposure to these molds as part of total load reduction. For the quicker we can unburden the total system, the easier it is to arrest the spreading phenomenon, which can cause irreversible damage.

Along with education in avoidance and environmental controls, attention to the diet, inhalant injections, and correction of identified nutrient deficiencies constitutes a solid treatment program for those not severely damaged by xeno-biotics. If the average chemically sensitive patient (if there is such a person), is tested for intracellular zinc, selenium, molybdenum, chromium, manganese, potassium, folate, and copper as well as magnesium and thiamine, it is usual for at least one—most often more than one—of these nutrients to be abnormally low.

When deficiencies are corrected, it is usual for other symptoms, in addition to those of overt chemical sensitivity, to improve. As an example, taurine is an amino acid that is commonly deficient in the chemically sensitive. It can also make a dramatic difference in treating resistant cardiac failure, seizures, recurrent infection or inflammation (Bland 1986). When one understands the biochemistry of detoxication, it is simple to see why taurine is often low in chemically sensitive people, as it is made in the body from cysteine. But cysteine is also a component of glutathione, a molecule of which is lost with every molecule of xenobiotic that is detoxified. As cysteine is consumed or wasted (as with daily pesticide exposures in commercial buildings, for example), this jeopardizes synthesis of taurine and the spreading phenomenon is set in motion. Multiple diverse symptoms then snowball.

Another amino acid, also a constituent of glutathione, is glycine. It has important roles of its own in the detoxication of toluene (outgassing from paints, for example), xylene (from solvents and adhesives like new carpet glue), and benzene (in gasoline, room deodorizers, etc.). It couples onto the metabolites of these xenobiotics and excretes them in the urine as hippuric acid, a measurable indicator of xenobiotic overload, or detoxication system exhaustion (Carlisle 1991). The point is, as one detox component like glutathione gets depleted, others like glycine suffer as well; this makes it clear why patient education (keeping the total load of exposures to a minimum) must be accompanied by nutrient assessment. Resolution of each aspect of the total load of the program enhances the others.

When correcting nutrient deficiencies, some take longer than others, as in minerals where a new enzyme needs to be made. Where trans fatty acids from margarines and hydrogenated corn oils have left the cell membranes defective, essential fatty acids must be replaced in order for proper cell function to resume. But through a careful diet history, an educated guess can be made regarding the cause of a deficiency. A therapeutic trial (for example, a change in a dietary oil) can save hundreds of dollars in expensive laboratory tests (see my *Tired or Toxic?*).

The Total Load Is Heightened by Delay in Diagnosis

A simple four-stage total load program can bring a respectable number of chemically sensitive people considerable relief within a few weeks or months. The program consists of:

1. Correction of the common nutrient deficiencies
2. Injections for molds (IMWR 1993), and other inhalants to which they were found to be sensitive
3. Instruction in a fundamental diet
4. Institution of environmental controls

Obviously, there is a broad range of damage to the detox pathways that will affect the speed and ease of recovery. It cannot be stressed enough that the earlier the recognition, the less likely is the patient to become severally disabled and an economic burden. Often these patients have had their diagnoses delayed by years of ineffective or exacerbating "treatment" by physicians untrained in the field.

Suppose an executive's detoxication system becomes compromised by too much alcohol, polyunsaturated oils (trans fatty acids) and repeated exposures to a pesticide at work. He then paints at home. By the time a new carpet is installed at work, he is a sitting duck and the only one to complain of severe chest pain, arrhythmia, headache, inability to concentrate, and depression with exhaustion. He may go on to get a flare-up of an old back injury, cancer of the prostate in several years, or a sudden fatal heart attack.

The very fact that these undetoxified xenobiotics can back up and cause symptoms in this man, suggests they have the potential to create damage in crucial cellular mechanisms (Miller 1987a). The longer his multiple undiagnosed deficiencies persist in the face of his continued unsuspected exposures, the greater the possibility of the involvement of a greater number of target organs with increasing severity of symptoms recalcitrant to medications.

SUMMARY

In this abbreviated attempt to simplify a complicated and variable disease, the best advice is to *first remove yourself from the offending substance.* For in order to heal, the detox system needs to rest. We do not prescribe tennis for recovery from bypass surgery. With a fracture, we immobilize it. These are all logical parts of the total load, to reduce the total burden to the body that is attempting to heal. And for the xenobiotic detoxication system, that means simply chemically clean air, clean food and clean water. Unfortunately, these are not always that easy to come by.

When removal from the source is not sufficiently curative or diagnostic because of more severe involvement, we then begin by unloading in additional ways: environmental controls, diet modifications, inhalant injections (specialized desensitizing materials) and nutrient deficiency corrections. There are many other components of treatment that I have omitted that are equally if not more important, depending on the individual case. This is an introduction, and courses, books and papers spell out the details. In the more severe cases, special programs of sauna (Rea 1992), and/or specialized diets are needed. When all else fails, specially designed environmentally controlled units are needed for the most severe cases to not only be diagnosed, but treated (Edgar 1979). And still we do not have all the answers, as this field is in its infancy.

Since chemical sensitivity was first described over 40 years ago by Dr. Theron Randolph, there is a great deal for the physician and the patient to learn. Nevertheless, there are simple and inexpensive techniques that can bring about remarkable improvements in the hands of physicians yet untrained in environmental medicine.

As you can begin to appreciate, *one cannot treat just the observed chemical sensitivity without addressing the entire health of the individual.* And it is just as well, since it is extremely rare to have chemical intolerance as one's sole complaint. And you know now that deficiencies and such also have a profound effect on the detoxication chemistry as well.

Thousands of metabolic defects in man have been documented in the medical literature to date. As well, there are thousands of references to substantiate the mechanism of chemical sensitivity (Rea 1992). But this knowledge is worthless while we operate under the paralyzing paradigm of drugs for all.

In essence, the diagnosis or name of the disease is really inconsequential, compared with identification of the biochemical and environmental causes. Often the diagnostic process becomes the treatment. We are evolving from a process that takes us from "diagnosis to drugs" (while waiting for another symptom to emerge) to an era in molecular medicine where finding the cause and correcting it enables far greater medical power over disease. By being forced into finding the answer to chemical sensitivity, we have simultaneously stumbled onto the biochemical and environmental causes of many diseases, including cancer (Miller 1987a). The era of molecular medicine is upon us.

We are truly ready for a paradigm shift in medicine. Out with drugs to merely hide symptoms, and more importantly, out with the passive patient. In order to get well, we must all become educated and become the pivotal member of our own successful medical team. The old medicine held us in good stead, but now leaves us powerless against chemical sensitivity, AIDS, arteriosclerosis and cancer, to name a few. For those of us so ill and limited in life by our chemical sensitivities, it was a nightmare, until we were forced to find out how to clear our environments.

It is now an exciting time in medicine. For at no other time have patients, through reading and education, had such an important and crucial role in determining their wellness.

REFERENCES

Barbeau A, Huxtable RJ: *TAURINE AND NEUROLOGICAL DISORDERS*, Raven Press, NY, 1987

Berglund B, Lindvall T, Mansson LG, (eds): *Healthy Buildings '88*. Swedish Council for Building Research, Stockholm, 1988

Bjarnson I, So A, Levi AJ, Peters TJ, Williams P, Zanelli GD, Gumpel JM, Ansell B: Intestinal permeability and inflammation in rheumatoid arthritis: effects of non-steroidal anti-inflammatory drugs. LANCET, 1171–1174, Nov 24, 1984

Bland J, (ed): *1984–1985: A YEAR IN NUTRITIONAL MEDICINE*, Keats Publishing, New Canaan, CT, 1986

Boyle E, et al: Chromium depletion in the pathogenesis of diabetes and arteriosclerosis, SOUTHERN MED J, 70:12, 1449–1453, Dec. 1977

Brasser LJ, Mulder WC, (eds): *Man and His Ecosystem, Proceedings of the 8th World Clean Air Congress 1989*. Vols. 1–4, Society for Clean Air in The Netherlands, P.O. B. 186, 2600 AD Delft, The Netherlands, 1989

Caldwell J, Jakoby WB: *Biological Basis of Detoxication*, Academic Press, NY, 1983

Carlisle EJF, Donnelly SM, Vasuvattakul S, Kamel KS, Tobe S, Halperin ML: Glue-sniffing and distal renal tubular acidosis: sticking to the facts, J AMER SOC NEPHROLOGY, 1:8, 1019–1027, 1991

Canada, *The 5th International Conference on Indoor Air Quality and Climate*, Vols. 1–5. Canada Mortgage and Housing Corp., Ottawa, Ontario, 1990

Cox IM, Campbell MJ, Dawson D: Red cell magnesium and chronic fatigue syndrome. LANCET, 337:757, 1991

Dager SR, et al: Panic disorder precipitated by exposure to organic solvents in the work place. AM J PSYCHIATRY, 144:8, 1056–1058, Aug, 1987

Edgar RT, Fenyves EJ, Rea WJ: Air pollution analysis used in operating an environmental control unit. ANN ALLERGY 42:3, 166–173, 1979

Elsborg L: The intake of vitamins and minerals by the elderly at home. INT J VIT NUTR RES, 53:321–329, 1983

EPA (Environmental Protection Agency): *Indoor Air Quality and Work Environment Study*, EPA Headquarters' Buildings Volume 1, Employee Survey. EPA Report 19K–1003, EPA, Washington DC, Nov. 1989

EPA: *Health Assessment Document for Toluene*, EPA-600/8–82–008F. U.S. EPA, Office of Health and environmental assessment, Washington DC 20460, August 1983

EPA: *The total exposure assessment methodology study*. Project summary. EPA/600/S6–87/002, U.S. EPA, Office of Acid Deposition, Environmental Monitoring and Quality Assurance, Washington DC, 20460, Sept. 1987

Feldman RG, Ricks NC, Baker EL: Neuropsychological effects of industrial toxins: A review. AM J IND MED. 1:211–227, 1980

Feuer G, de la Inglesia FA: *MOLECULAR BIOCHEMISTRY OF HUMAN DISEASE*, VOL III, CRC Press, Boca Raton FL, p319, 1990

Frei B, England L, Ames B: Ascorbate is an outstanding antioxidant in human blood plasma. PROC NATL ACAD SCI, 86: 6377–6381, 1989

Frezza M, DiPadova C, Pozzato G, Terpin M, Baraona E, Lieber CS: High blood alcohol levels in women: The role of decreased gastric alcohol dehydrogenase activity and first-pass metabolism. NEW ENGL J MED, 322:2, 95–99, Jan 11, 1990

Gershon S: Psychiatric sequelae of chronic exposure to organophosphorus insecticides. LANCET, 1371–1374, June 24, 1961

Gorbach SL: Function of the normal human microflora. SCAND J INFECT DIS SUPPL 49:17–30, 1986

Gupta KC, Ulsamer AG, Preuss PW: Formaldehyde in indoor air: Sources and toxicity. In: *International Symposium on Indoor Air Pollution, Health and Energy Conservation*. Harvard University Press, Boston, MA, 1981

Halstead CH, Rucker RB, (eds): *Nutrition and the Origin of Disease*. Academic Press, NY, 278, 1989

Hunnisett A, Howard J, Davies S: Gut fermentation (or the "autobrewery") syndrome: a new clinical test with initial observations and discussion of clinical and biochemical implications. J NUTR RES, 1:33–38, 1990

IMWR: Acute pancreatitis following cutaneous exposure to an organophosphate insecticide. INT MED WORLD REP p10, Mar 1–14, 1989

IMWR: The tight building syndrome and the nose. INT MED WORLD REP, p25–27, Feb 1993

IMWR: Pericardial effusion and constrictive pericarditis caused by asbestos exposure. INT MED WORLD REP, 16:21, 16, Nov 15–30, 1991

Jackson PG, Baker RW, Lessof MH, Ferret J, MacDonald DM: Intestinal permeability in patients with eczema and food allergy. LANCET 1:1285–1286, 1981

Jeffries W, *SAFE USES OF HYDROCORTISONE,* Charles C Thomas Co., Springfield IL, 1981

King WP, Rubin WA, Fadal RG, Ward WA, Trevino RJ, Pierce WB, Stewart JA, Boyles JH: Provocation-neutralization: A two-part study. Part I. The intracutaneous provocative food test: A multi-center comparison study. OTOLARYNGOL HEAD NECK SURG, 99:3, 263–272, Sept. 1988a

King, et al, ibid, Part II: Subcutaneous neutralization therapy: A multi-center study. pp 272–278, 1988b

King WP: The role of the skin end point titration method in allergy: In: Goldman JL, (ed), *THE PRINCIPLES AND PRACTICE OF RHINOLOGY.* John Wiley & Sons, NY, 283–292, 1987

Klaasen CD, Amdur MO, Doull J, (eds): *Cassarett and Doull's Toxicology, the Basic Science of Poisons,* 3rd ed., MacMillan Publishing Co., NY, 1986

Kokkonen, et al: Impaired gastric function in children with cow's milk intolerance. EUR J PED 132;1, 1979

LaVia MF, LaVia DS: Phenol derivatives are immunosuppressive in mice. DRUG & CHEM TOXICOL, 2;167–177, 1979

Levin SL: Behavioral effects of organophosphate pesticides in man. CLIN TOX, 9:3, 391–405, 1976

Levine SA: *ANTI-OXIDANT ADAPTATION, ITS ROLE IN FREE RADICAL PATHOLOGY,* Allergy Research Group, San Leandro, CA, 1985

Linder MC, (ed): *NUTRITIONAL BIOCHEMISTRY AND METABOLISM WITH CLINICAL APPLICATIONS.* Elsevier, NY, 1984

Lockey JE, et al: Progressive systemic sclerosis associated with exposure to trichloroethylene. J OCCUP MED, 29:6, 493–496, 1987

Mago L: The effects of industrial chemicals on the heart. In: Balazo T, (ed), *CARDIAC TOXICOLOGY,* CRC Press, Boca Raton, pp206–207, 1981

Mensink RP, Katan MB: Effect of dietary trans-fatty acids on high-density and low-density lipoprotein cholesterol levels in healthy subjects. N ENGL J MED, 323:7, 439–445, Aug 16, 1990

Miller JB, et al: Mechanisms of chemical carcinogenesis. CANCER, 47:5, 1055–1064, Mar 1987a

Miller JB: Intradermal provocative-neutralizing food testing and subcutaneous food extract injection therapy. In: *FOOD ALLERGY AND INTOLERANCE,* Brostoff J, Challacombe SJ, (eds), Bailliere Tindall, London 932–946, 1987b

Miller JB: A double-blind study of food extract injection therapy: a preliminary report. AN ALLERGY, 38:3, 185–191, 1977

Mullin GE: Food allergy and irritable bowel syndrome. JAMA, 265:13, 1736, Apr 3, 1991

CHEMICAL SENSITIVITY / 45

Nalebuff DJ: Allergen immunotherapy in the management of allergic rhinitis, in Goldman JL, (ed), *THE PRINCIPLES AND PRACTICE OF RHINOLOGY.* John Wiley & Sons, NY, 269–281, 1988

Nour-Eldin F: Preliminary report: Uptake of phenol by vascular and brain tissue. MICROVASCULAR RESEARCH, 2:224–225, 1970

Padh H: Vitamin C: Newer insights into its biochemical functions. NUTR REV 49:3, 65–70, Mar 1991

Parke DV: Activation mechanisms to chemical toxicity. ARCH TOXICOL: 60:5–15, 1987

Prilipko LL, et al: Activation of lipid peroxidation: a mechanism triggering autoimmune response. ACTA PHYSIOL PHARMACOL BULG, 9:4, 14–50, 1983

Randolph TG: Sensitivity to petroleum, including its derivatives and antecedents. J LAB MED, 40:931–932, 1952

Rapp DJ: *IS THIS YOUR CHILD?* William Morrow Co., NY 1991

Rapp DJ: Double-blind confirmation and treatment of milk-sensitivity. MED J AUST 1:571–572, 1978

Raunskov G, et al: Glomerulonephritis in exposure to organic solvents. ACTA MEDI SCAND, 205:575–579, 1979

Rea WJ, Bell IB, Suits CW, Smiley RE: Food and chemical susceptibility after environmental chemical overexposure: case histories. ANN ALLERGY, 41:2, 101–107, Aug 1987a

Rea WJ: Environmentally triggered cardiac disease. ANN ALLERGY, 40:4, 243–251, 1978b

Rea WJ: Recurrent environmentally triggered thrombophlebitis: A five-year follow-up. ANN ALLERGY, 47:333–344, Part I, Nov 1981

Rea WJ, Podell RN, Williams M, Fenyves I, Sprague DE, Johnson AR: Elimination of oral food challenge reaction by injection of food extracts. A double-blind evaluation. ARCH OTOLARYNGOL, 110:248–252, 1984

Rea WJ: Cardiovascular disease in response to chemicals and foods. In: *FOOD ALLERGY AND INTOLERANCE,* Brostoff J, Challacombe SJ, (eds), Bailliere Tindall, Philadelphia, 737–753, 1987b

Rea WJ: *CHEMICAL SENSITIVITY.* Vol I, CRC Press, Boca Raton, 1992

Reilly PM, Schiller HJ, Bulkley GB: Reactive oxygen metabolites in shock: IV TRAUMA. SCIENTIFIC AMERICAN, 1991

Rogers SA: A thirteen month work, leisure, sleep environmental fungal survey. ANN ALLERGY, 52:338–341, 1984

Rogers SA: *THE E.I. SYNDROME,* Prestige Publishing, Syracuse, NY, 1986

Rogers SA: Diagnosing the tight building syndrome. ENVIRON HEALTH PERSPECT, 76: 195–198, 1987

Rogers, SA: Unrecognized magnesium deficiency masquerades as diverse symptoms: Evaluation of an oral magnesium challenge test. INT CLIN NUTR REV, 11:3, 117–125, 1991a

Rogers SA: Indoor fungi as part of the cause of recalcitrant symptoms of the tight building syndrome. ENVIRON INTERN, 17:4, 271–276, 1991

Rogers SA: Zinc deficiency as a model for developing chemical sensitivity. INT CLIN NUTR REV, 12:1, 253–259, 1989

Rousseau D, Rea WJ, Enwright J: *YOUR HOME AND YOUR HEALTH AND WELL-BEING.* Hartley & Marks Publishing, Vancouver BC, 1987

Stamler R et al: Cardiac status after four years in a trial on nutritional therapy for high blood pressure. ARCH INTERN MED, 149: 661–665, Mar 1989

Stortebecker P: *MERCURY POISONING FROM DENTAL AMALGAM, A HAZARD TO HUMAN BRAIN.* Bio-Probe, Inc, POB 58010, Orlando, FL, 32858–0160, 1986

Teahon K, Smethurst P, Pearson M, Levi AJ, Bjarnason I: The effect of elemental diet on intestinal permeability and inflammation in Crohn's disease. GASTROENTEROLOGY, 101:84–89, 1991

CPSIA information can be obtained
at www.ICGtesting.com
Printed in the USA
BVHW090045090722
641728BV00014B/1519

9 780879 836344